Idioms & Phrases in American Sign Language Volume 1

―――――――――――――

Teacher's Workbook

―――――――――――――

First Edition :: Spring 2009

Best when in use with Idioms & Phrases in American Sign Language, Volume 1: DVD

Written & Developed by Gilda Ganezer and Avery Posner

© 2009. Everyday ASL Productions. All rights reserved.

Table of Contents

Category	Page #
Introduction	3
1st Class - Idioms # 1-7	4-9
2nd Class - Idioms # 8-14	10-15
3rd Class - Idioms # 15-21	16-26
4th Class - Idioms # 22-28	27-32
5th Class - Idioms # 29-35	33-38
6th Class - Idioms # 36-42	39-54
7th Class - Idioms # 43-52	55-60
8th Class – Final Review	61-67
Index	68-74
Order Form	75

Idioms & Phrases in American Sign Language – Introduction

Every language contains idioms and phrases used by people of all ages and cultures. This video was created by a team of Deaf ASL experts at Everyday ASL Productions, whose teaching experience and curriculum development has paved the way to accurately translate idioms and phrases into American Sign Language along with complex forms of Deaf Culture. This includes the use of facial expressions and body movements which help to convey the true meaning of these expressions themselves.

Communication and cultural gaps will diminish by learning these expressions; and will help to build a strong rapport between the Deaf/Hard-of-Hearing and hearing peers.

This video is excellent for Deaf and Hard-of-Hearing children as well as interpreters, teachers, parents and many professionals using American Sign Language to communicate clearly and naturally. This video has also been developed for students and teachers from secondary and post secondary schools as well as colleges and universities to use in all sorts of courses promoting American Sign Language.

Additional Idioms & Phrases in American Sign Language videos and curriculum will follow, and you can learn more about them by visiting our website at www.everydayasl.com.

1st Class - Idioms # 1-7

1st Class - Lesson Plan
(40 minutes – 1½ hours)

Step 1: Introduce yourself and briefly explain your teaching experience

Step 2: Explain to the students the purpose of this course and why it is beneficial

    a) Just like any other spoken language, ASL users, ranging from young children to adults, incorporate idioms and phrases in everyday conversations. These environments usually take place in various parts of the Deaf community, at one's home, event outings, schools, gatherings, online videos, the workplace, counseling sessions and much more

    b) This course is excellent for interpreters, families, teachers, students and young people

    c) Every idiom and phrase taught in class will include appropriate use of facial expressions, fluency, sign location, handshapes and palm orientation (show several examples)

    d) Students in this course will learn how to translate English idioms and phrases into ASL and vice versa correctly without losing the true meaning, feeling and/or concept

    e) Ultimately, learning idioms will promote both hearing and Deaf communities to develop a better understanding of one another and thus, the communication barrier will be a thing of the past

Step 3: Student Introductions – have the students introduce themselves

Step 4: Provide <u>Idioms & Phrases in American Sign Language</u> DVDs to students

Step 5: Copy and hand out **Idioms # 1-7** Worksheet (page 7)

Step 6: Teach students each idiom / phrase

    a) Remember to focus on one idiom / phrase at a time

    b) After handing out the worksheets be sure to clearly show students how to sign each idiom / phrase and make sure they incorporate handshapes, facial expressions and hand movements

    c) Have each student sign the idiom / phrase and make sure s/he expresses them correctly

    d) Show students how to sign the idiom / phrase in a sentence. Use the same sentence example seen in the worksheet and DVD

    e) Have each student sign the sentence back to you and continue to look for correct use of facial expressions, handshapes and fluency with the whole sentence

Step 7: Homework Assignments:

1. Students should review **Idioms # 1-7** from the **Idioms & Phrases in American Sign Language, Volume 1** DVD

2. Students should practice by creating **new sentence examples** for every one of these idioms along with one of the topics listed below:

    FOOD, FAMILY, WEATHER, CLOTHES and/or SCHOOL

3. Students should prepare to show one of their new sentence examples for the next class

Homework Assignment: Idioms # 1-7 Worksheet

Practice DVD: Idioms & Phrases in ASL, Vol. 1 - Chapter 1: Idioms # 1-7

	Idiom / Phrase	Sentence Example in English	ASL Glosses*
1	an ASL pro / proficient in ASL	I have been taking ASL classes for the past seven years. Today, I am an ASL pro!	ME TAKE-UP+++ ASL CLASSES SINCE 7-YEARS NOW ME ASL-HIGH-SPEED
2	as easy as pie, piece of cake	Rollerskating was a piece of cake for me when I was a little girl, but forget about me doing it today!	LONG-TIME-AGO ME LITTLE GIRL ROLLERSKATING PIECE-OF-CAKE NOW FORGET-IT
3	at a loss for words / speechless	The teacher told me off, and thus I was at a loss for words. Nonetheless I learned something!	TEACHER IX TALK LAST-WORD ME GASP BUT (HAND) ME LEARN SOMETHING
4	awesome / remarkable / "big" wow!	The Deaf theater group is really awesome at showing many facial expressions. It's a big wow!	DEAF THEATRE KNACK FACIAL EXPRESSION EXPRESSIVE AWESOME
5	back up	It is important to back up the computer every week.	COMPUTER BACKUP EVERY-WEEK IMPORTANT
6	barely / hardly / scarcely / hard to come by	I only had five dollars left and was barely able to shop!	ME HAVE 5-DOLLAR LEFT, ME SHOPPING BARELY
7	better than nothing	The refrigerator only had an apple left. I felt it was better than nothing and ate it.	REFRIGERATOR HAVE 1 APPLE, (MOUTH: THAT'S-ALL), BETTER-THAN-NOTHING ME TAKE-IT-ATE-IT-UP

Notes:

* - **What is an ASL Gloss?** ASL Gloss is when you would transcribe or write down signs in text form. Remember that when you gloss, you are not translating the language but you are attempting to transcribe it Word for word or sign for sign. Some ASL Glosses will contain notations to show more information about use of fingerspelling, facial and/or body movements while signing the sentence.

Tips: "+++" means the word is signed more than 2-3 times. "mouth" is where you would show mouth-movement only. Any words you see that are shown grouped with a hyphen "-" are shown in one word sign; "BETTER-THAN-NOTHING" only has one sign, not three.

Notes

Notes

2nd Class - Idioms # 8-14

2nd Class - Lesson Plan
(40 minutes – 1½ hours)

Step 1: Roll Call (check attendance)

Step 2: **Review Idioms # 1-7** with new sentence examples

    a) Have students review one idiom at a time

    b) Correct students' sign production (handshape, palm orientation, location and movement)

    c) Ask first student to pick any idiom to show how to use it in a new sentence

    d) Correct student's sentence production

    e) Have the class copy the sentence

    f) If you have a large class, additional students can repeat the idiom but with new sentence examples

Step 3: Copy and hand out **Idioms # 8-14** Worksheet (page 13)

Step 4: Teach students each idiom / phrase

    a) Remember to focus on one idiom / phrase at a time

    b) After handing out the worksheets be sure to show students how to sign each idiom / phrase and make sure they incorporate handshapes, facial expressions and hand movements

    c) Have each student sign the idiom / phrase and you make sure s/he expresses it correctly

Idioms & Phrases in American Sign Language, Volume 1: Teacher's Workbook

d) Show students how to sign the idiom / phrase in a sentence. Use the same sentence example seen in the worksheet and DVD

e) Have each student sign the sentence back to you and continue to look for correct use of facial expressions, handshapes and fluency with the whole sentence

Step 5: **Homework Assignments:**

1. Students should review **Idioms # 8-14** from the DVD

2. Students should practice by creating **new sentence examples** for every one of these idioms along with one of the topics listed below:

    ENTERTAINMENT, SPORTS, HOBBIES, HEALTH and/or CLOTHES

3. Students should prepare to show one of their new sentence examples for the next class

Homework Assignment: Idioms # 8-14 Worksheet
Practice DVD: Idioms & Phrases in ASL, Vol. 1 - Chapter 2: Idioms # 8-14

	Idiom / Phrase	Sentence Example in English	ASL Glosses*
8	blow someone away	Just as soon as I got the exam papers, I was blown away because it was a hard test!	TEST PAPER-CLASSIFER-TO-FACE ME LOOK-IT HARD ME BLEW-AWAY-FACE
9	came to mind	The food list that you made for me came to mind. Can you please give it to me now as I am ready to go shopping.	WAVE-CALLING MIND-POPUP BEFORE FOOD YOU MAKE-A-LIST NOW ME READY GO-TO SHOPPING PLEASE GIVE-ME
10	chip in	You know how bosses can be so cranky sometimes? **Well, last week at the Halloween party our staff agreed to chip in and buy our boss a new hat.** Now he is in a better mood! Whew! Oh, we already have the video – do you want to see it? Go ahead and take a look!†	YOU-KNOW BOSS IX-THEY TEND-TO CRANKY-UP **ANYWAY LAST-WEEK HALLOWEEN PARTY WE STAFF DISCUSS AGREE CHIP-IN GIVE NEW HAT** NOW IX BETTER MOOD WHEW WE ALREADY VIDEO-CAMERA WANNA SEE - GO-RIGHT-AHEAD
11	close call, by one's hair, that was really close	I remembered how that bus almost hit me. Whew, what a close call!	ME REMEMBER HAPPEN ME WALK BUS PASS-BY-CLASSIFIER CLOSE-CALL
12	common sense	If you are not sure about something, using common sense or instinct is important.	IF NOT SURE, IMPORTANT USE COMMON-SENSE OR INSTINCT
13	compulsive liar	I don't like the politician because that person is a compulsive liar.	THAT POLITICIAN ME NOT+LIKE WHY IX STRONG+COMPULSIVE-LIAR
14	conceited, egomaniac	Boy, this man has been showing off his new motorcycle. What an egomaniac!	MAN SHOW-OFF HIS NEW MOTORCYCLE, IX EGOMANIAC!

Notes:

* **- What is an ASL Gloss?** ASL Gloss is when you would transcribe or write down signs in text form. Remember that when you gloss, you are not translating the language but you are attempting to transcribe it Word for word or sign for sign. Some ASL Glosses will contain notations to show more information about use of fingerspelling, facial and/or body movements while signing the sentence.

† - Since the sentence seen in the video is longer than average, let's only focus on the **bold and underlined words** as sentence practice.

Tips: Any words you see that are shown grouped with a hyphen "-" are shown in one word sign; "BETTER-THAN-NOTHING" only has one sign, not three. Any "+" symbols between two words are called compound signs where you would sign word for word to denote a single word. "IX" is an acronym for "index" which is when one points to a third party with an index finger.

Notes

Notes

3rd Class - Idioms # 15-21

3rd Class - Lesson Plan
(40 minutes – 1½ hours)

Step 1: Roll Call (check attendance)

Step 2: **Review Idioms # 8-14** with new sentence examples

    a) Have students review one idiom at a time

    b) Correct students' sign production (handshape, palm orientation, location and movement)

    c) Ask first student to pick any idiom and to show how to use it in a new sentence

    d) Correct student's sentence production

    e) Have the class to copy the sentence

    f) If you have a large class, additional students can repeat the idiom but with new sentence examples

Step 3: Breakaway Activity: IdiomWord Game
(similar to the old TV game show "Password")

Purpose:

    a) develop conversational and communication skills between students

    b) help each student express idioms and phrases more freely

    c) develop student's respect, awareness and appreciation towards idioms that are highly used throughout parts of the Deaf Community

Game instructions:

1. Make a copy of the IdiomWord card sheet (page 19-20) and cut out the cards ahead of time (before class). Pair two of the same cards together as one of each will be given to each team

2. Split the class into two teams (if you have 8 students, for example, create team A with 4 students and team B with another 4 students)

3. Two students from team A and another two students from team B are called to the front of the class. The rest of the other students stay in their seats as the audience to watch and observe the game in action

4. Give one IdiomWord card to one student from team A and the other SAME IdiomWord card to one student from team B

5. Start the game with team A, where the student with the card can only use a few words to hint at what his word is, to the other student in the team

6. Only 1 guess is allowed and if the student guesses an idiom correctly, s/he scores a point. However, if the student gives a wrong idiom, then team B takes their turn to continue the game until the correct answer is made

7. When one of the teams reaches 3 points, stop the game and switch students in the audience

8. The game then resumes until either one of the teams reaches 6 points to win the game

9. Suggestion: you can distribute treats (i.e. candy, lollipops, etc.) at end of the game as rewards

10. Bonus for teachers: You will see two pages of <u>IdiomWord Helpful Clues & Hints</u> (page 21-22) that should help you show students in the game how to improve their hints with different vocabulary words with similar meanings of the idiom / phrase. You will notice that the hints and clues are in ASL glosses which will help you show the students how to express these hints

IdiomWord Cards
(make a copy of both sheets and cut out into cards)

an ASL pro, proficient in ASL	an ASL pro, proficient in ASL
as easy as pie, piece of cake	as easy as pie, piece of cake
at a loss for words, speechless	at a loss for words, speechless
awesome, remarkable, "big" wow!	awesome, remarkable, "big" wow!
back up	back up
barely, hardly, scarcely, hard to come by	barely, hardly, scarcely, hard to come by
better than nothing	better than nothing

IdiomWord Cards
(make a copy of both sheets and cut out into cards)

blow someone away	blow someone away
came to mind	came to mind
chip in	chip in
close call, by one's hair, that was really close	close call, by one's hair, that was really close
common sense	common sense
compulsive liar	compulsive liar
conceited, egomaniac	conceited, egomaniac

IdiomWord Helpful Clues & Hints

(This is for the teacher, these hints are helpful for students to use)

IDIOM	HINTS / CLUES (in ASL Glosses)
an ASL pro, proficient in ASL	SIGN GOOD, SIGN FAST, SIGN SMOOTH
as easy as pie, piece of cake	EASY, NOT HARD, EASY PASS, NO PROBLEM
at a loss for words, speechless	QUIET DOWN, NO MORE TALK
awesome, remarkable, "big" wow!	WOW, WONDERFUL, GREAT
back up	SAVE INFORMATION, PRESERVE INFORMATION
barely, hardly, scarcely, hard to come by	NOT COMMON, VERY FEW, RARE-fs
better than nothing	HAVE LITTLE LEFT, HAVE SOME LEFT, ONLY ONE LEFT

IdiomWord Helpful Clues & Hints
(This is for the teacher, these hints are helpful for students to use)

IDIOM	HINTS / CLUES (in ASL Glosses)
blow someone away	UNEXPECTED, REAL SHOCK
came to mind	REMEMBER, REMEMBER SOMETHING, NOW ME REMEMBER
chip in	PAY HALF, SHARE PAY, HELP PAY 1/2
close call, by one's hair, that was really close	ALMOST, NEAR MISS, VERY NEAR, MISS BY 1 INCH
common sense	SMART, CLEVER, USE YOUR HEAD STREET SMART
compulsive liar	NOT HONEST, ALWAYS LIE, TALK NOT TRUE
conceited, egomaniac	SHOW-OFF, BIG-HEADED, THINK WONDERFUL

Step 4: Copy and hand out students **Idioms # 15-21** Worksheet (page 24)

    a) Remember to focus on one idiom / phrase at a time

    b) After handing out the worksheets be sure to show students how to sign each idiom / phrase and make sure they incorporate handshapes, facial expressions and hand movements

    c) Have each student sign the idiom / phrase and make sure they express them correctly

    d) Show students how to sign the idiom / phrase in a sentence. Use the same sentence example seen in the worksheet and DVD

    e) Have each student sign the sentence back to you and continue to look for correct use of facial expressions, handshapes and fluency with the whole sentence

Step 5: **Homework Assignments:**

    1. Students should review **Idioms # 15-21** from the DVD

    2. Students should do further practice by creating **new sentence examples** for every one of these idioms along with one of the topics listed below:

        RELATIONSHIP, POLITICS, CURRENT EVENTS, PETS and/or JOBS

    3. Students should prepare to show one of their new sentence examples for the next class

Homework Assignment: Idioms # 15-21 Worksheet
Practice DVD: Idioms & Phrases in ASL, Vol. 1 - Chapter 3: Idioms # 15-21

	Idiom / Phrase	Sentence Example in English	ASL Glosses*
15	darn you	You have been teasing and scaring me. Darn you!	YOU TEASE-ME++ ME SCARE++ SICK-FOOL YOU
16	defeat, wipe out	At the tournament, my basketball team wiped out the other team!	BASKETBALL TOURNAMENT MY TEAM WIPE-OUT-OTHER-TEAM
17	dirty business	We have been shuffling around our hard-earned income and now they want to increase the rent. What a dirty business!	TWO-OF-US MONEY-AROUND IX RENT INCREASE DIRTY BUSINESS HUH (GESTURE)
18	don't feel like	I don't feel like throwing out the garbage.	GARBAGE ME THROW-OUT DONT-FEEL-LIKE
19	dumbfounded	I was dumbfounded when my best friend brought 5 dogs. How could we clean up after them?	MY BEST-FRIEND BRING 5 DOGS ME DUMBFOUNDED WHY-RHQ CLEAN HOW?
20	fall back, relapse	My diet was perfect for 3 months until I saw a delicious chocolate candy bar. Now I am suffering from a relapse in my diet.	ME DIET SINCE 3-MONTHS PERFECT HAPPEN ME SAW CHOCOLATE ME DROOL ME FALL-BACK!
21	feebleminded	You are trying to fool me. Don't do that, I'm not feebleminded!	YOU TRY-fs FOOL-ME, ME FEEBLE-MINDED ("1"-FINGER-wave-gesture) NO-NO

Notes:

* - **What is an ASL Gloss?** ASL Gloss is when you would transcribe or write down signs in text form. Remember that when you gloss, you are not translating the language but you are attempting to transcribe it Word for word or sign for sign. Some ASL Glosses will contain notations to show more information about use of fingerspelling, facial and/or body movements while signing the sentence.

Tips: "+++" means the word is signed more 2-3 times. "fs" is short for fingerspelled word. As a variation, you are to sign the word "TRY" in a fingerspelled loan sign form. Any words you see that are shown grouped with a hyphen "-" are shown in one word sign; For example "BETTER-THAN-NOTHING" only has one sign, not three.

Notes

Notes

4th Class - Idioms # 22-28

4th Class - Lesson Plan
(40 minutes – 1½ hours)

Step 1: Roll Call (check attendance)

Step 2: Review Idioms # 15-21 with new sentence examples

    a) Have students review one idiom at a time

    b) Correct students' sign production (handshape, palm orientation, location and movement)

    c) Ask first student to pick any idiom and to show how to use it in a new sentence

    d) Correct student's sentence production

    e) Have the class to copy the sentence

    f) If you have a large class, additional students can repeat the idiom but with new sentence examples

Step 3: Facial Expression Correction & Receptive Skills Activity

    a) Explain why facial expressions are important grammatical features in American Sign Language.

        • it provides more information about feelings/emotions and/or the situation

        • it matches the true meaning of the idiom and sentence itself

        • without using facial expressions, there would be no meaning to the idiom!

    b) Then you, as a teacher, will pick any one of the idioms / phrases from **#15-21** and show **NO** facial expressions while signing the idiom in front of a student. Let that student help you by showing you the correct facial expression along with signs for that idiom / phrase

c) Continue this activity with the rest of the class

Step 4: Copy and hand out **Idioms # 22-28** Worksheet (page 30)

Step 5: Teach students each idiom / phrase

a) Remember to focus on one idiom / phrase at a time

b) After handing out the worksheets be sure to show students how to sign each idiom / phrase and make sure they incorporate handshapes, facial expressions and hand movements

c) Have each student sign the idiom / phrase and you make sure he expresses it correctly

d) Show students how to sign the idiom / phrase in a sentence. Use the same sentence example seen in the worksheet and DVD

e) Have each student sign the sentence back to you and continue to look for correct use of facial expressions, handshapes and fluency with the whole sentence

Step 6: Homework Assignments:

1. Students should review **Idioms # 22-28** from the DVD

2. Students should practice by creating **new sentence examples** for every one of these idioms along with one of the topics listed below:
   **VACATION, HOLIDAY, HOME LIFE,
   EDUCATION and/or TRANSPORTATION**

3. Students should prepare to show one of their new sentence examples for the next class

Homework Assignment: Idioms # 22-28 Worksheet
Practice DVD: Idioms & Phrases in ASL, Vol. 1 - Chapter 4: Idioms # 22-28

	Idiom / Phrase	Sentence Example in English	ASL Glosses*
22	financially broke	I've been paying for the house mortgage and car repairs. Now I'm broke!	HOUSE MORTGAGE, CAR REPAIR ME TWO-HANDS-SPEND-FLOW++ ME BROKE
23	gross someone out	The new restaurant serves yucky food that grossed me out!	RESTAURANT IX NEW FORM BUT IX FOOD GROSS
24	gut feeling	I have a gut feeling that it will rain tomorrow.	ME GUT FEELING TOMORROW RAIN
25	hey, what's up, what's your problem	You have been talking against me, what's up with that?	YOU TALK AGAINST-ME++ WHAT'S-UP
26	hit the jackpot	I felt as if I hit the jackpot finding this gorgeous apartment after lengthy searches.	APARTMENT ME LOOK-FOR++ HIT-THE-JACKPOT FOUND GORGEOUS
27	holy cow, whoa	My family; the five of us, visited New York City and saw many tall skyscraper buildings. Holy cow!	MY FAMILY FIVE-OF-US GO-TO VISIT NYC-fs WE SAW MANY BUILDINGS CH-TALL-classifier HOLY-COW!
28	if I were you, if I were in your shoes	Oh, you want to withdraw from college? Well, if I were you I would stay there because of the scholarship.	YOU WANT WITHDRAW COLLEGE RH-Q IF ME-WERE-YOU ME STAY-THERE WHY RH-Q THEY OFFER SCHOLARSHIP

Notes:

* - **What is an ASL Gloss?** ASL Gloss is when you would transcribe or write down signs in text form. Remember that when you gloss, you are not translating the language but you are attempting to transcribe it Word for word or sign for sign. Some ASL Glosses will contain notations to show more information about use of fingerspelling, facial and/or body movements while signing the sentence.

Tips: "+++" means the word is signed more 2-3 times. Any words you see that are shown grouped with a hyphen "-" are shown in one word sign; "BETTER-THAN-NOTHING" only has one sign, not three.

Notes

Notes

5th Class - Idioms # 29-35

5th Class - Lesson Plan
(40 minutes – 1½ hours)

Step 1: **Roll Call (check attendance)**

Step 2: **Review Idioms # 22-28** with new sentence examples

    a) Have students review one idiom at a time

    b) Correct students' sign production (handshape, palm orientation, location and movement)

    c) Ask first student to pick any idiom and to show how to use it in a new sentence

    d) Correct student's sentence production

    e) Have the class to copy the sentence

    f) If you have a large class, additional students can repeat the idiom but with new sentence examples

Step 3: **Fluency Correction & Receptive Skills Activity**

    a) Explain how fluency is important in American Sign Language.

        • it provides natural flow of expression about feelings/emotions and/or the situation

        • it prevents distraction of thought processes from viewers

        • signing faster or slower does not gain any advantages and natural speed is more important

    b) Then you, as a teacher, will pick any one of the idioms / phrases from **# 1-28** and show an **INCORRECT** level of fluency (too fast, too slow, too choppy) while signing the idiom in front of a student. Let that student help you by showing you the correct fluency for that idiom / phrase

c) Continue this activity with the rest of the class

Step 4: Copy and hand out **Idioms # 29-35** Worksheet (page 36)

Step 5: Teach students each idiom / phrase

a) Remember to focus on one idiom / phrase at a time

b) After handing out the worksheets be sure to show students how to sign each idiom / phrase and make sure they incorporate handshapes, facial expressions and hand movements

c) Have each student sign the idiom / phrase and you make sure s/he expresses them correctly

d) Show students how to sign the idiom / phrase in a sentence. Use the same sentence example seen in the worksheet and DVD

e) Have each student sign the sentence back to you and continue to look for correct use of facial expressions, handshapes and fluency with the whole sentence

Step 6: **Homework Assignments:**

1. Students should review **Idioms # 29-35** from the DVD

2. Students should practice by creating **new sentence examples** for every one of these idioms along with one of the topics listed below:
   ENTERTAINMENT, WEATHER, HEALTH, JOBS and/or CURRENT EVENTS

3. Students should prepare to show one of their new sentence examples for the next class

Homework Assignment: Idioms # 29-35 Worksheet
Practice DVD: Idioms & Phrases in ASL, Vol. 1 - Chapter 5: Idioms # 29-35

	Idiom / Phrase	Sentence Example in English	ASL Glosses*
29	in one ear and out the other	My doctor ordered me to stop smoking. Well, his words went in one ear and out the other!	MY DOCTOR ORDERED-ME STOP SMOKING ME IN-ONE-EAR-OUT-THE-OTHER
30	it is of no significance, despite, regardless of	Despite the car accident, it is important that you are OK.	CAR ACCIDENT DESPITE IMPORTANT YOU OK
31	jump for joy	I am jumping for joy because I got an iPod from a grab bag at the Christmas party.	CHRISTMAS PARTY YOU KNOW++ GRAB BAG ME WHAT-IS-IT-RH-Q IPOD ME JUMP-JOY YES!
32	jump to conclusions	Wait! Don't jump to conclusions. Let me explain first.	WAIT! YOU JUMP-TO-CONCLUSION HOLD-ON-WAVE LET ME EXPLAIN FIRST
33	keep an eye on	Whoa, I really love the new car! I'm going to keep my eye on it!	NEW CAR-fs ME LOVE-IT WHOA (Y-HANDSHAPE) ME KEEP-AN-EYE-ON-IT
34	live and learn, roll with the punches	After attending a Deaf school while living in a hearing world, I have learned to roll with the punches. As a result, I am able to blend into both worlds.	ME GROW-UP DEAF SCHOOL HEARING WORLD (CONTRASTIVE STRUCTURE) ME ROLL-WITH-THE-PUNCHES NOW ME BLENDED-IN CAN ME
35	lost in thought	Uhh, I was lost in thought. What was I talking about?	HEY UHHH LOST-IN-THOUGHT WHAT ME TALKING-ABOUT (additional dialogue follows)

Notes:

* - **What is an ASL Gloss?** ASL Gloss is when you would transcribe or write down signs in text form. Remember that when you gloss, you are not translating the language but you are attempting to transcribe it Word for word or sign for sign. Some ASL Glosses will contain notations to show more information about use of fingerspelling, facial and/or body movements while signing the sentence.

Tips: "+++" means the word is signed more 2-3 times. "mouth" is where you would show mouth-movement only. Any words you see that are shown grouped with a hyphen "-" are shown in one word sign; "BETTER-THAN-NOTHING" only has one sign, not three.

Notes

Notes

6th Class - Idioms # 36-42

6th Class - Lesson Plan
(40 minutes – 1½ hours)

Step 1: **Roll Call (check attendance)**

Step 2: **Review Idioms # 29-35** with new sentence examples

    a) Have students review one idiom at a time

    b) Correct students' sign production (handshape, palm orientation, location and movement)

    c) Then ask first student to pick any idiom and to show how to use it in a new sentence

    d) Correct student's sentence production

    e) Ask class to copy the sentence

    f) If you have a large class, additional students can repeat the idiom but with new sentence examples

Step 3: **Breakaway Activity: Idiom Bingo Game**
            (similar to the well-known Bingo game)

Purpose:

    a) develop receptive and correlation skills between students

    b) help each student identify and differentiate idioms and phrases

    c) further develop student's respect, awareness and appreciation towards idioms that are highly used throughout parts of the Deaf Community

    d) refresh students' practice on idioms # 1-35

Game instructions:

1. Make a copy of the <u>Idiom Bingo Cards # 1-20</u> seen in the following pages and cut out the cards ahead of time (before class)

2. Make a copy of the <u>Idiom Bingo Caller Cards</u>, seen in the following pages and cut out the cards ahead of time (before class)

3. Briefly introduce and explain the purpose and rules of the game (the purposes are outlined in a previous page)

4. Give one unique Idiom Bingo Card to each student

5. You, as a teacher, keep all the Idiom Bingo Caller Cards. Shuffle the Caller Cards and then place them facing down on the your desk

6. Have each student watch you select one card from all the Caller Cards on the desk and sign the idiom only twice

7. Let each student see which matching idiom is available on their cards and mark them off

8. Continue steps 6-7 until a student has reached a winning pattern. The winning pattern can either be vertical, horizontal or diagonal.

Winning Pattern Examples:

I	D	I	O	M
an ASL pro	blow someone away	dam you	conceited	defeat, wipe out
dirty business	as easy as pie	came to mind	better than nothing	don't feel like
dumb-founded	close call	FREE SPACE	chip in	fall back, relapse
feeble-minded	barely, hardly	common sense	at a loss for words	financially broke
back up	gross someone out	compulsive liar	gut feeling	awesome

I	D	I	O	M
an ASL pro	blow someone away	dam you	conceited	defeat, wipe out
dirty business	as easy as pie	came to mind	better than nothing	don't feel like
dumb-founded	close call	FREE SPACE	chip in	fall back, relapse
feeble-minded	barely, hardly	common sense	at a loss for words	financially broke
back up	gross someone out	compulsive liar	gut feeling	awesome

I	D	I	O	M
an ASL pro	blow someone away	dam you	conceited	defeat, wipe out
dirty business	as easy as pie	came to mind	better than nothing	don't feel like
dumb-founded	close call	FREE SPACE	chip in	fall back, relapse
feeble-minded	barely, hardly	common sense	at a loss for words	financially broke
back up	gross someone out	compulsive liar	gut feeling	awesome

Step 4: Copy and hand out **Idioms # 36-42** Worksheet (page 52)

Step 5: Teach students each idiom / phrase

    a) Remember to focus on one idiom / phrase at a time

    b) After handing out the worksheets be sure to show students how to sign each idiom / phrase and make sure they incorporate handshapes, facial expressions and hand movements

    c) Have each student sign the idiom / phrase and make sure they express them correctly

    d) Show students how to sign the idiom / phrase in a sentence. Use the same sentence example seen in the worksheet and DVD

    e) Have each student sign the sentence back to you and continue to look for correct use of facial expressions, handshapes and fluency with the whole sentence

Step 6: **Homework Assignments:**

    1. Students should review **Idioms # 36-42** from the DVD

    2. Students should practice by creating **new sentence examples** for every one of these idioms along with one of the topics listed below:

        FOOD, SCHOOL EDUCATION, SPORTS, MONEY and/or HOBBIES

    3. Students should prepare to show one of their new sentence examples for the next class

Idiom Bingo Cards # 1-20 (make one copy of all cards and cut out each card)

IDIOM BINGO CARD # 1

I	D	I	O	M
an ASL pro	blow someone away	darn you	conceited	defeat, wipe out
dirty business	as easy as pie	came to mind	better than nothing	don't feel like
dumb-founded	close call	FREE SPACE	chip in	fall back, relapse
feeble-minded	barely, hardly	common sense	at a loss for words	financially broke
back up	gross someone out	compulsive liar	gut feeling	awesome

IDIOM BINGO CARD # 2

I	D	I	O	M
in one ear and out the other	darn you	financially broke	don't feel like	keep an eye on
hit the jackpot	despite	gross someone out	holy cow	if I were in your shoes
chip in	came to mind	FREE SPACE	back up	fall back, relapse
piece of cake	blow someone away	gut feeling	jump for joy	what's up
live and learn	defeat, wipe out	lost in thought	dirty business	jump to conclusions

IDIOM BINGO CARD # 3

I	D	I	O	M
roll with the punches	Feeble-minded	came to mind	dirty business	keep an eye on
blow someone away	jump for joy	compulsive liar	regardless of	chip in
close call	dumb-founded	FREE SPACE	don't feel like	better than nothing
hard to come by	darn you	an ASL pro	defeat, wipe out	common sense
back up	in one ear and out the other	conceited, egomaniac	fall back, relapse	lost in thought

IDIOM BINGO CARD # 4

I	D	I	O	M
came to mind	chip in	that was really close	if I were you	conceited, ego-maniac
what's your problem	an ASL pro	as easy as pie	speechless	in one ear and out the other
hit the jackpot	blow someone away	FREE SPACE	"big" wow!	it is of no significance
holy cow, whoa	better than nothing	hardly	back up	jump for joy
financially broke	gross someone out	gut feeling	compulsive liar	common sense

Idioms & Phrases in American Sign Language, Volume 1: Teacher's Workbook   visit www.everydayasl.com   43

IDIOM BINGO CARD # 5

I	D	I	O	M
an ASL pro	piece of cake	speechless	remarkable	back up
scarcely	better than nothing	blow someone away	came to mind	chip in
by one's hair	common sense	FREE SPACE	hit the jackpot	egomaniac
darn you	wipe out	dirty business	don't feel like	jump for joy
relapse	feeble-minded	financially broke	gross someone out	gut feeling

IDIOM BINGO CARD # 6

I	D	I	O	M
lost in thought	live and learn	keep an eye on	jump to conclusions	jump for joy
if I were in your shoes	whoa	what's your problem	gut feeling	gross someone out
feeble-minded	relapse	FREE SPACE	don't feel like	wipe out
common sense	close call	chip in	came to mind	blow someone away
better than nothing	hard to come by	back up	awesome	at a loss for words

IDIOM BINGO CARD # 7

I	D	I	O	M
an ASL pro	as easy as pie	at a loss for words	blow someone away	came to mind
chip in	darn you	wipe out	dirty business	don't feel like
dumb-founded	fall back	FREE SPACE	financially broke	gross someone out
gut feeling	what's up	hit the jackpot	in one ear and out the other	despite
jump for joy	jump to conclusions	keep an eye on	live and learn	lost in thought

IDIOM BINGO CARD # 8

I	D	I	O	M
better than nothing	common sense	darn you	wipe out	don't feel like
relapse	at a loss for words	lost in thought	live and learn	whoa
gross someone out	financially broke	FREE SPACE	as easy as pie	back up
close call	blow someone away	hardly	an ASL pro	gut feeling
hit the jackpot	in one ear and out the other	it is of no significance	keep an eye on	came to mind

Idioms & Phrases in American Sign Language, Volume 1: Teacher's Workbook

IDIOM BINGO CARD # 9

I	D	I	O	M
fall back, relapse	despite	gross someone out	holy cow	if I were in your shoes
what's up	piece of cake	blow someone away	gut feeling	jump for joy
jump to conclusions	came to mind	FREE SPACE	back up	in one ear and out the other
darn you	close call	don't feel like	keep an eye on	hit the jackpot
live and learn	defeat, wipe out	lost in thought	dirty business	chip in

IDIOM BINGO CARD # 10

I	D	I	O	M
an ASL pro	blow someone away	dirty business	as easy as pie	defeat, wipe out
conceited	defeat, wipe out	better than nothing	don't feel like	keep an eye on
at a loss for words	financially broke	FREE SPACE	dumb-founded	close call
barely, hardly	common sense	darn you	chip in	fall back, relapse
gut feeling	awesome	came to mind	back up	gross someone out

IDIOM BINGO CARD # 11

I	D	I	O	M
dirty business	keep an eye on	hard to come by	close call	dumb-founded
regardless of	chip in	back up	darn you	an ASL pro
don't feel like	better than nothing	FREE SPACE	in one ear and out the other	conceited, egomaniac
defeat, wipe out	common sense	roll with the punches	Feeble-minded	came to mind
fall back, relapse	lost in thought	blow someone away	jump for joy	compulsive liar

IDIOM BINGO CARD # 12

I	D	I	O	M
holy cow, whoa	better than nothing	hardly	"big" wow!	it is of no significance
financially broke	gross someone out	gut feeling	back up	jump for joy
that was really close	if I were you	FREE SPACE	came to mind	chip in
as easy as pie	speechless	conceited, egomaniac	what's your problem	an ASL pro
compulsive liar	common sense	in one ear and out the other	hit the jackpot	blow someone away

Idioms & Phrases in American Sign Language, Volume 1: Teacher's Workbook   visit www.everydayasl.com

IDIOM BINGO CARD # 13

I	D	I	O	M
scarcely	better than nothing	blow someone away	by one's hair	common sense
speechless	came to mind	chip in	darn you	wipe out
an ASL pro	piece of cake	FREE SPACE	relapse	feeble-minded
dirty business	don't feel like	jump for joy	remark-able	back up
financially broke	gross someone out	gut feeling	hit the jackpot	egomaniac

IDIOM BINGO CARD # 14

I	D	I	O	M
relapse	don't feel like	feeble-minded	hard to come by	back up
close call	came to mind	common sense	jump to conclusions	jump for joy
better than nothing	wipe out	FREE SPACE	gut feeling	gross someone out
keep an eye on	awesome	at a loss for words	lost in thought	live and learn
what's your problem	chip in	blow someone away	if I were in your shoes	whoa

IDIOM BINGO CARD # 15

I	D	I	O	M
gut feeling	what's up	an ASL pro	as easy as pie	at a loss for words
jump for joy	jump to conclusions	chip in	darn you	wipe out
blow someone away	came to mind	FREE SPACE	gross someone out	financially broke
dirty business	don't feel like	despite	dumb-founded	fall back
keep an eye on	live and learn	lost in thought	hit the jackpot	in one ear and out the other

IDIOM BINGO CARD # 16

I	D	I	O	M
as easy as pie	back up	darn you	close call	blow someone away
an ASL pro	gut feeling	lost in thought	hit the jackpot	in one ear and out the other
keep an eye on	came to mind	FREE SPACE	better than nothing	common sense
wipe out	don't feel like	hardly	relapse	at a loss for words
live and learn	whoa	it is of no significance	gross someone out	financially broke

Idioms & Phrases in American Sign Language, Volume 1: Teacher's Workbook   visit www.everydayasl.com

IDIOM BINGO CARD # 17

I	D	I	O	M
jump to conclusions	fall back, relapse	despite	gross someone out	holy cow
darn you	piece of cake	blow someone away	gut feeling	hit the jackpot
if I were in your shoes	came to mind	FREE SPACE	back up	chip in
jump for joy	close call	don't feel like	keep an eye on	what's up
in one ear and out the other	live and learn	defeat, wipe out	lost in thought	dirty business

IDIOM BINGO CARD # 18

I	D	I	O	M
better than nothing	don't feel like	keep an eye on	conceited	defeat, wipe out
an ASL pro	blow someone away	dirty business	as easy as pie	defeat, wipe out
at a loss for words	financially broke	FREE SPACE	dumb-founded	close call
barely, hardly	common sense	darn you	chip in	fall back, relapse
gut feeling	awesome	came to mind	back up	gross someone out

IDIOM BINGO CARD # 19

I	D	I	O	M
an ASL pro	blow someone away	darn you	conceited	defeat, wipe out
dirty business	as easy as pie	came to mind	in one ear and out the other	don't feel like
keep an eye on	hard to come by	FREE SPACE	awesome	fall back, relapse
holy cow, whoa	better than nothing	feeble-minded	"big" wow!	it is of no significance
financially broke	gross someone out	gut feeling	back up	jump for joy

1IDIOM BINGO CARD # 20

I	D	I	O	M
as easy as pie	speechless	conceited, egomaniac	what's your problem	an ASL pro
compulsive liar	common sense	in one ear and out the other	hit the jackpot	blow someone away
lost in thought	fall back, relapse	FREE SPACE	darn you	chip in
an ASL pro	if I were in your shoes	roll with the punches	Feeble-minded	defeat, wipe out
dirty business	jump for joy	came to mind	better than nothing	don't feel like

Idioms & Phrases in American Sign Language, Volume 1: Teacher's Workbook   visit www.everydayasl.com

Idiom Bingo Caller Cards

(make a copy of all idioms and cut out into cards – THIS IS FOR TEACHER USE ONLY)

an ASL pro / proficient in ASL	as easy as pie, piece of cake	at a loss for words / speechless
awesome / remarkable / "big" wow!	back up	Barely, hardly, scarcely, hard to come by
better than nothing	blow someone away	came to mind

chip in	close call, by one's hair, that was really close	common sense
compulsive liar	conceited, egomaniac	darn you
defeat, wipe out	dirty business	don't feel like

dumbfounded	fall back, relapse	feebleminded
financially broke	gross someone out	gut feeling
hey, what's up, what's your problem	hit the jackpot	holy cow, whoa

if I were you, if I were in your shoes	in one ear and out the other	it is of no significance, despite, regardless of
jump for joy	jump to conclusions	keep an eye on
live and learn, roll with the punches	lost in thought	SURPRISE! YOU PICK ANY IDIOM!

Homework Assignment: Idioms # 36-42 Worksheet
Practice DVD: Idioms & Phrases in ASL, Vol. 1 - Chapter 6: Idioms # 36-42

	Idiom / Phrase	Sentence Example in English	ASL Glosses*
36	make a fuss	I have been making a fuss with my artwork simply because I want to do a perfect job.	ART ME alt-FUSS++ WHY-RHQ ME WANT PERFECT JOB
37	messed up	You kept changing the subject and I am messed up and confused!	YOU TALK CHANGE++ ME HEAD-MESSED-UP
38	much better than someone	I do dance much better than this person however she sings better than I do. It's true...It's true!	ME DANCE BETTER-THAN-PERSON BUT SICK-TWIST IX SING BETTER-THAN-ME TRUE+BUSINESS TRUE+BUSINESS
39	on the fence, ambivalent	I have been accepted by two colleges but I am on the fence as to which choice to make.	TWO COLLEGE ACCEPT OFFER-OFFER-ME (alternating signs) ME NOT SURE WHICH ME AMBIVALENT
40	overlook	I cannot find the post office. Maybe I overlooked it.	ME CANT FIND POST OFFICE, ME OVERLOOK MAYBE ME
41	pro, expert, experienced	This person is an expert graphic designer. Where did he go to school to learn that?	GRAPHIC DESIGN IX PRO, IX GO-TO SCHOOL LEARN WHERE? (Wh-word Question)
42	rarely	I've been preaching to my daughter but she rarely listens to me.	MY DAUGHTER ME PREACH-HER++ IX LISTEN HARDLY

Notes:

* - What is an ASL Gloss? ASL Gloss is when you would transcribe or write down signs in text form. Remember that when you gloss, you are not translating the language but you are attempting to transcribe it Word for word or sign for sign. Some ASL Glosses will contain notations to show more information about use of fingerspelling, facial and/or body movements while signing the sentence.

Tips: "+++" means the word is signed more 2-3 times. "mouth" is where you would show mouth-movement only. Any words you see that are shown grouped with a hyphen "-" are shown in one word sign; "BETTER-THAN-NOTHING" only has one sign, not three. RHQ is short for Rhetorical Question is an ASL sentence structure, which includes lowering the eyebrows and holding the Wh-word little longer at the end of the sentence.

Notes

Notes

7th Class - Idioms # 43-52

7th Class - Lesson Plan
(40 minutes – 1½ hours)

Step 1: **Roll Call (check attendance)**

Step 2: **Review Idioms # 36-42** with new sentence examples

    a) Have students review one idiom at a time

    b) Correct students' sign production (handshape, palm orientation, location and movement)

    c) Ask first student to pick any idiom and to show how to use it in a new sentence

    d) Correct student's sentence production

    e) Ask class to copy the sentence

    f) If you have a large class, additional students can repeat the idiom but with new sentence examples

Step 3: **Sign Parameters & Receptive Skills Activity**

    a) Explain how 4 parameters are important in American Sign Language

- these 4 parameters are:
    1. handshape
    2. palm orientation
    3. location
    4. movement

- these parameters are easily overlooked by others; therefore this exercise will teach every student to be more receptive and aware of how to use every parameter for all idioms correctly

- even the "slightest" sign inaccuracies can lead to a misunderstanding

b) Then you, as a teacher, will pick any one of the idioms / phrases from **# 1-42** and show an **INCORRECT** handshape (one of four parameters) when signing the idiom in front of a student. Let that student help you by showing you the correct handshape for that idiom / phrase and also show you the idiom in that full sentence with the correct handshape

c) Continue this activity with the rest of the class and be sure to show only one wrong parameter per student

Step 4: Copy and hand out **Idioms # 43-52** Worksheet (page 58)

Step 5: Teach students each idiom / phrase

a) Remember to focus on one idiom / phrase at a time

b) After handing out the worksheets be sure to clearly show students how to sign each idiom / phrase and make sure they incorporate handshapes, facial expressions and hand movements

c) Have each student sign the idiom / phrase and make sure s/he expresses them correctly

d) Show students how to sign the idiom / phrase in a sentence. Use the same sentence example seen in the worksheet and DVD

e) Have each student sign the sentence back to you and continue to look for correct use of facial expressions, handshapes and fluency with the whole sentence

Step 6: **Homework Assignments:**

1. Students should review **Idioms # 43-52** from the DVD

2. Students should practice by creating **new sentence examples** for every one of these idioms along with any topics

3. Students should prepare to show one of their new sentence examples for the next / final class

Homework Assignment: Idioms # 43-52 Worksheet
Practice DVD: Idioms & Phrases in ASL, Vol. 1 - Chapter 7: Idioms # 43-52

	Idiom / Phrase	Sentence Example in English	ASL Glosses*
43	stinky, it really stinks	The movie I rented last night really stinks!	LAST NIGHT ME BORROW-FROM MOVIE IX STINKY
44	taking advantage of (negatively)	Don't take advantage of the horse by any means. Remember, we love horses.	HORSE YOU TAKE-ADVANTAGE-NEGATIVELY WAVE-NO, WE LOVE HORSES
45	that's not what I'm talking about, not what I mean	I didn't mean to suggest cancelling the meeting as I only wanted to postpone it. That's all!	MEETING ME CANCEL NOT-TALK-ABOUT ME WANT-TO POSTPONE THAT'S-ALL
46	that's understandable	The classes were cancelled due to much snow. That's understandable!	SNOW BIG ("cha" mouth movement) CLASSES CANCEL THAT'S-UNDERSTANDABLE
47	to talk on and on	We've been talking on and on about it. Now let's get right to the point!	WE-BOTH TALK ON-AND-ON NOT PAY-fs** BETTER POINT
48	totally, mostly, utmost	Today, I notice that ASL education has totally spread out. Wow!	NOW ME NOTICE ASL LEARN++ SPREAD-OUT CHAMP WOW-fs
49	wide-awake, alert	I drank seven cups of coffee and now I am really wide-awake!	ME DRINK 7 COFFEE FINISH NOW ME WIDE-AWAKE
50	word on the street, through the grapevine	Word on the street tells me that you are going to get married next month. Is this true?	RUMOR YOU MARRY NEXT MONTH TRUE+BUSINESS?
51	worship, idolize	I idolize children and animals and, oh wait, stuffed animals, too!	ME WORSHIP CHILDREN, ANIMALS WAIT STUFFED ANIMALS TOO
52	you're crazy	You are going to eat the whole pizza pie? You're crazy!	YOU EAT WHOLE PIZZA CRAZY YOU

Notes:

* - **What is an ASL Gloss?** ASL Gloss is when you would transcribe or write down signs in text form. Remember that when you gloss, you are not translating the language but you are attempting to transcribe it Word for word or sign for sign.

Tips: "fs" is short for fingerspelled loan sign. Any words you see that are shown grouped with a hyphen "-" are shown in one word sign; "BETTER-THAN-NOTHING" only has one sign, not three.

Notes

Notes

8th Class - Idioms # 1-52
Review / Final

8th Class - Lesson Plan
(40 minutes – 1½ hours)

Step 1: Roll Call (check attendance)

Step 2: Review Idioms # 43-52 with new sentence examples

    a) Have students review one idiom at a time

    b) Correct students' sign production (handshape, palm orientation, location and movement)

    c) Ask first student to pick any idiom and to show how to use it in a new sentence

    d) Correct student's sentence production

    e) Have the class to copy the sentence

    f) If you have a large class, additional students can repeat the idiom but with new sentence examples

Step 3: Cumulative Review Idioms # 1-52

    a) review all previous worksheets beginning with # 1

    b) review each and every idiom / phrase with the entire class

    c) be sure all parameters are correctly used

    d) time permitting, review all previous sentences beginning with # 1

Step 4: How to Maintain Use of These Idioms

a) explain how important it is to interact with Deaf people of all age groups and not to be "afraid" to try using these idioms and phrases

b) recommendations and ideas on how to meet with Deaf people:

- inviting them to class

- meeting them at any social gatherings (coffee shops or malls)

- volunteering at a festival or fund-raising event

- attending a film festival (organized by Deaf filmmakers)

- posting a vlog on Youtube or any one of the video-sharing networking platforms online

c) Explain the importance of continuing to learn idioms and everyday phrases by taking the next course in Idioms & Phrases in ASL (volume / level 2, 3, 4, etc.).

Step 5: BONUS Final Exam Assignment (only if necessary, this is good for the 9th or final class meet):

1. review idioms 1-52 on their DVDs

2. develop a brief 1 to 2 minute ASL Storytelling including at least 4-5 idioms for the final

3. only as an option, each student presentation can be videotaped by you, as a teacher, to be used for grading or as an ASL storytelling keepsake for each student to take home and review

Notes

Notes

Notes

Notes

Idioms / Phrases (Vol. 1) # 1-52 English Index

	English	Sentence Example in English	Sentence Example in ASL Glosses	Chapter
1	an ASL pro / proficient in ASL	I have been taking ASL classes for the past seven years. Today, I am an ASL pro!	ME TAKE-UP+++ ASL CLASSES SINCE 7-YEARS NOW ME ASL-HIGH-SPEED	1
2	as easy as pie, piece of cake	Rollerskating was a piece of cake for me when I was a little girl, but forget about me doing it today!	LONG-TIME-AGO ME LITTLE GIRL ROLLERSKATING PIECE-OF-CAKE NOW FORGET-IT	1
3	at a loss for words / speechless	The teacher told me off, and thus I was at a loss for words. Nonetheless I learned something!	TEACHER IX TALK LAST-WORD ME GASP BUT (HAND) ME LEARN SOMETHING	1
4	awesome / remarkable / "big" wow!	The Deaf theater group is really awesome at showing many facial expressions. It's a big wow!	DEAF THEATRE KNACK FACIAL EXPRESSION EXPRESSIVE AWESOME	1
5	back up	It is important to back up the computer every week.	COMPUTER BACKUP EVERY-WEEK IMPORTANT	1
6	barely / hardly / scarcely / hard to come by	I only had five dollars left and was barely able to shop!	ME HAVE 5-DOLLAR LEFT, ME SHOPPING BARELY	1
7	better than nothing	The refrigerator only had an apple left. I felt it was better than nothing and ate it.	REFRIGERATOR HAVE 1 APPLE, (MOUTH: THAT'S-ALL), BETTER-THAN-NOTHING ME TAKE-IT-ATE-IT-UP	1

Idioms & Phrases in American Sign Language, Volume 1: Teacher's Workbook

8	blow someone away	Just as soon as I got the exam papers, I was blown away because it was a hard test!	TEST PAPER-CLASSIFER-TO-FACE ME LOOK-IT HARD ME BLEW-AWAY-FACE	2
9	came to mind	The food list that you made for me came to mind. Can you please give it to me now as I am ready to go shopping.	WAVE-CALLING MIND-POPUP BEFORE FOOD YOU MAKE-A-LIST NOW ME READY GO-TO SHOPPING PLEASE GIVE-ME	2
10	chip in	You know how bosses can be so cranky sometimes? Well, last week at the Halloween party our staff agreed to chip in and buy our boss a new hat. Now he is in a better mood! Whew! Oh, we already have the video – do you want to see it? Go ahead and take a look!†	YOU-KNOW BOSS IX-THEY TEND-TO CRANKY-UP ANYWAY LAST-WEEK HALLOWEEN PARTY WE STAFF DISCUSS AGREE CHIP-IN GIVE NEW HAT NOW IX BETTER MOOD WHEW WE ALREADY VIDEO-CAMERA WANNA SEE - GO-RIGHT-AHEAD	2
11	close call, by one's hair, that was really close	I remembered how that bus almost hit me. Whew, what a close call!	ME REMEMBER HAPPEN ME WALK BUS PASS-BY-CLASSIFIER CLOSE-CALL	2
12	common sense	If you are not sure about something, using common sense or instinct is important.	IF NOT SURE, IMPORTANT USE COMMON-SENSE OR INSTINCT	2
13	compulsive liar	I don't like the politician because that person is a compulsive liar.	THAT POLITICAN ME NOT+LIKE WHY IX STRONG+COMPULSIVE-LIAR	2
14	conceited, egomaniac	Boy, this man has been showing off his new motorcycle. What an egomaniac!	MAN SHOW-OFF HIS NEW MOTORCYCLE, IX EGOMANIAC!	2

15	darn you	You have been teasing and scaring me. Darn you!	YOU TEASE-ME++ ME SCARE++ SICK-FOOL YOU	3
16	defeat, wipe out	At the tournament, my basketball team wiped out the other team!	BASKETBALL TOURNAMENT MY TEAM WIPE-OUT-OTHER-TEAM	3
17	dirty business	We have been shuffling around our hard-earned income and now they want to increase the rent. What a dirty business!	TWO-OF-US MONEY-AROUND IX RENT INCREASE DIRTY BUSINESS HUH (GESTURE)	3
18	don't feel like	I don't feel like throwing out the garbage.	GARBAGE ME THROW-OUT DONT-FEEL-LIKE	3
19	dumbfounded	I was dumbfounded when my best friend brought 5 dogs. How could we clean up after them?	MY BEST-FRIEND BRING 5 DOGS ME DUMBFOUNDED WHY-RHQ CLEAN HOW?	3
20	fall back, relapse	My diet was perfect for 3 months until I saw a delicious chocolate candy bar. Now I am suffering from a relapse in my diet.	ME DIET SINCE 3-MONTHS PERFECT HAPPEN ME SAW CHOCOLATE ME DROOL ME FALL-BACK!	3
21	feebleminded	You are trying to fool me. Don't do that, I'm not feebleminded!	YOU TRY-fs FOOL-ME, ME FEEBLE-MINDED ("1"-FINGER-wave-gesture) NO-NO	3

Idioms & Phrases in American Sign Language, Volume 1: Teacher's Workbook

22	financially broke	I've been paying for the house mortgage and car repairs. Now I'm broke!	HOUSE MORTGAGE, CAR REPAIR ME TWO-HANDS-SPEND-FLOW++ ME BROKE	4
23	gross someone out	The new restaurant serves yucky food that grossed me out!	RESTAURANT IX NEW FORM BUT IX FOOD GROSS	4
24	gut feeling	I have a gut feeling that it will rain tomorrow.	ME GUT FEELING TOMORROW RAIN	4
25	hey, what's up, what's your problem	You have been talking against me, what's up with that?	YOU TALK AGAINST-ME++ WHAT'S-UP	4
26	hit the jackpot	I felt as if I hit the jackpot finding this gorgeous apartment after lengthy searches.	APARTMENT ME LOOK-FOR++ HIT-THE-JACKPOT FOUND GORGEOUS	4
27	holy cow, whoa	My family; the five of us, visited New York City and saw many tall skyscraper buildings. Holy cow!	MY FAMILY FIVE-OF-US GO-TO VISIT NYC-fs WE SAW MANY BUILDINGS CH-TALL-classifier HOLY-COW!	4
28	if I were you, if I were in your shoes	Oh, you want to withdraw from college? Well, if I were you I would stay there because of the scholarship.	YOU WANT WITHDRAW COLLEGE RH-Q IF ME-WERE-YOU ME STAY-THERE WHY RH-Q THEY OFFER SCHOLARSHIP	4

Idioms & Phrases in American Sign Language, Volume 1: Teacher's Workbook   visit www.everydayasl.com

29	in one ear and out the other	My doctor ordered me to stop smoking. Well, his words went in one ear and out the other!	MY DOCTOR ORDERED-ME STOP SMOKING ME IN-ONE-EAR-OUT-THE-OTHER	5
30	it is of no significance, despite, regardless of	Despite the car accident, it is important that you are OK.	CAR ACCIDENT DESPITE IMPORTANT YOU OK	5
31	jump for joy	I am jumping for joy because I got an iPod from a grab bag at the Christmas party.	CHRISTMAS PARTY YOU KNOW++ GRAB BAG ME WHAT-IS-IT-RH-Q IPOD ME JUMP-JOY YES!	5
32	jump to conclusions	Wait! Don't jump to conclusions. Let me explain first.	WAIT! YOU JUMP-TO-CONCLUSION HOLD-ON-WAVE LET ME EXPLAIN FIRST	5
33	keep an eye on	Whoa, I really love the new car! I'm going to keep my eye on it!	NEW CAR-fs ME LOVE-IT WHOA (Y-HANDSHAPE) ME KEEP-AN-EYE-ON-IT	5
34	live and learn, roll with the punches	After attending a Deaf school while living in a hearing world, I have learned to roll with the punches. As a result, I am able to blend into both worlds.	ME GROW-UP DEAF SCHOOL HEARING WORLD (CONTRASTIVE STRUCTURE) ME ROLL-WITH-THE-PUNCHES NOW ME BLENDED-IN CAN ME	5
35	lost in thought	Uhh, I was lost in thought. What was I talking about?	HEY UHHH LOST-IN-THOUGHT WHAT ME TALKING-ABOUT (additional dialogue follows)	5

Idioms & Phrases in American Sign Language, Volume 1: Teacher's Workbook

#	Idiom	Sentence	ASL Gloss	Ch.
36	make a fuss	I have been making a fuss with my artwork simply because I want to do a perfect job.	ART ME alt-FUSS++ WHY-RHQ ME WANT PERFECT JOB	6
37	messed up	You kept changing the subject and I am messed up and confused!	YOU TALK CHANGE++ ME HEAD-MESSED-UP	6
38	much better than someone	I do dance much better than this person however she sings better than I do. It's true...It's true!	ME DANCE BETTER-THAN-PERSON BUT SICK-TWIST IX SING BETTER-THAN-ME TRUE+BUSINESS TRUE+BUSINESS	6
39	on the fence, ambivalent	I have been accepted by two colleges but I am on the fence as to which choice to make.	TWO COLLEGE ACCEPT OFFER-OFFER-ME (alternating signs) ME NOT SURE WHICH ME AMBIVALENT	6
40	overlook	I cannot find the post office. Maybe I overlooked it.	ME CANT FIND POST OFFICE, ME OVERLOOK MAYBE ME	6
41	pro, expert, experienced	This person is an expert graphic designer. Where did he go to school to learn that?	GRAPHIC DESIGN IX PRO, IX GO-TO SCHOOL LEARN WHERE? (Wh-word Question)	6
42	rarely	I've been preaching to my daughter but she rarely listens to me.	MY DAUGHTER ME PREACH-HER++ IX LISTEN HARDLY	6

43	stinky, it really stinks	The movie I rented last night really stinks!	LAST NIGHT ME BORROW-FROM MOVIE IX STINKY	7
44	taking advantage of (negatively)	Don't take advantage of the horse by any means. Remember, we love horses.	HORSE YOU TAKE-ADVANTAGE-NEGATIVELY WAVE-NO, WE LOVE HORSES	7
45	that's not what I'm talking about, not what I mean	I didn't mean to suggest cancelling the meeting as I only wanted to postpone it. That's all!	MEETING ME CANCEL NOT-TALK-ABOUT ME WANT-TO POSTPONE THAT'S-ALL	7
46	that's understandable	The classes were cancelled due to much snow. That's understandable!	SNOW BIG ("cha" mouth movement) CLASSES CANCEL THAT'S-UNDERSTANDABLE	7
47	to talk on and on	We've been talking on and on about it. Now let's get right to the point!	WE-BOTH TALK ON-AND-ON NOT PAY-fs** BETTER POINT	7
48	totally, mostly, utmost	Today, I notice that ASL education has totally spread out. Wow!	NOW ME NOTICE ASL LEARN++ SPREAD-OUT CHAMP WOW-fs	7
49	wide-awake, alert	I drank seven cups of coffee and now I am really wide-awake!	ME DRINK 7 COFFEE FINISH NOW ME WIDE-AWAKE	7
50	word on the street, through the grapevine	Word on the street tells me that you are going to get married next month. Is this true?	RUMOR YOU MARRY NEXT MONTH TRUE+BUSINESS?	7
51	worship, idolize	I idolize children and animals and, oh wait, stuffed animals, too!	ME WORSHIP CHILDREN, ANIMALS WAIT STUFFED ANIMALS TOO	7
52	you're crazy	You are going to eat the whole pizza pie? You're crazy!	YOU EAT WHOLE PIZZA CRAZY YOU	7

Idioms & Phrases in American Sign Language, Volume 1: Teacher's Workbook   visit www.everydayasl.com

Contact: Support Department
Everyday ASL Productions, Ltd.
Tel: 866-485-1785 V/TTY/VP / Fax: 631-980-3967
Email: support@everydayasl.com / Website: http://everydayasl.com
PMB 212, 169 Commack Road, Suite H, Commack, NY 11725

Idioms & Phrases in American Sign Language
Teacher's Curriculum Kit Order Form

Please fill out the form thoroughly or order online at **http://everydayasl.com**

Full Name:	
Organization Name:	
Address:	

City:		State / Prov.:		Zip Code:	
Phone:			Email:		

Description	Quantity	Unit Price	Total
Option 1: **Idioms & Phrases in American Sign Language, Volume 1** **Teacher's Kit Only** Includes: 1 Teacher's Workbook 1 Teacher's Instructional DVD		$ 39.95*	

Option 2:
Idioms & Phrases in American Sign Language, Volume 1
Complete Kit
 	
Includes: 1 Teacher's Workbook,
               1 Teacher's Instructional DVD
               4 Student DVDs and
               2 additional Student DVDs (FREE)
		$ 69.95*	

NY State resident(s) add sales tax of 8.625%			
Shipping & Handling for Teacher's Kit Only - $ 7.99 (additional kits, add $ 3 each)			
Shipping & Handling for Complete Kit - $ 9.99 (additional kits, add $ 4 each)			
GRAND TOTAL			

Make all money orders or checks payable to: **EVERYDAY ASL PRODUCTIONS, LTD**.

Mail payment to: **Everyday ASL Productions, PMB 212, 169 Commack Rd, Suite H, Commack, NY, 11725**

All orders will be shipped within 4-6 weeks after receiving checks/money orders. To process your order more timely, you can buy them online at http://everydayasl.com

* - at time of this publication, Everyday ASL Productions, Ltd. reserves the right to adjust prices at anytime, where necessary.

Made in the USA
Charleston, SC
25 February 2014